doodle BUGS

RP | KIDS

PHILADELPHIA · LONDON

By Nikalas Catlow

First published in Great Britain by Buster Books,
an imprint of Michael O'Mara Books Limited, 2009

First published in the United States
by Running Press Book Publishers, 2010

Printed in Canada

9 8 7 6 5 4 3 2 1
Digit on the right indicates the number of this printing

ISBN 978-0-7624-3762-7

Illustrated by Nikalas Catlow

This edition published by Running Press Kids,
an imprint of
Running Press Book Publishers
2300 Chestnut Street
Philadelphia, PA 19103-4371

Visit us on the web!
www.runningpress.com

The world of creepy crawlies is a wriggly,
slimy, itchy, scratchy one.
There are bugs of all shapes and sizes.

There are insects,
such as beautiful
butterflies and bees.

There are eight-legged
arachnids, such as
scuttling spiders.

There are others,
too, such as wiggly
worms, millipedes,
and snails.

You'll find them all in this book.

Here are more of the bugs you'll find
in this book. Can you copy them?

an ant

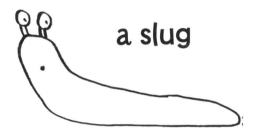
a slug

a snail

a dragonfly

a beetle

a scorpion

a butterfly

a stick insect

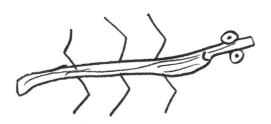

All insects have six legs.
Can you add legs to this one?

Can I have shoes, too?

Insects use antennae on their heads to feel and smell things. Add their antennae.

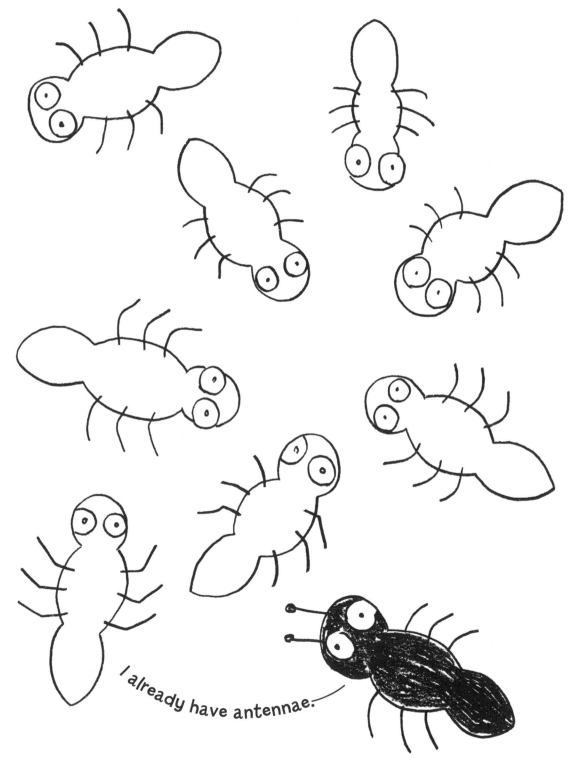

I already have antennae.

Draw the scariest spider ever, and make Mom scream!

Some bugs fly towards lights.
What bugs are buzzing around this bulb?

Bugs love sweet, sticky things.
What is buzzing around this honey pot?

Different butterflies have differently shaped wings.

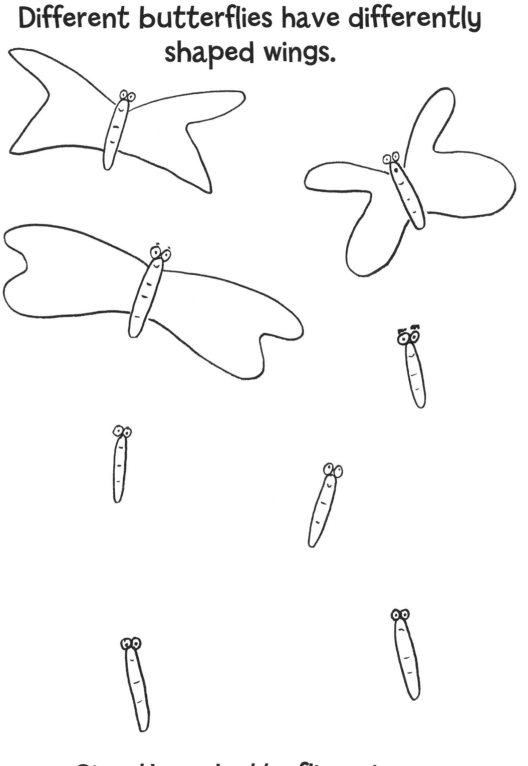

Give these butterflies wings.

Snails carry shells on their backs.
Complete these snails.

I hide in my shell when I'm scared.

Flowers make a sugary liquid called nectar, which bees love to drink. Fill the flowers with thirsty bees.

A beetle called a whirligig beetle
has very special eyes.

Its eyes can see what is above the water. . .

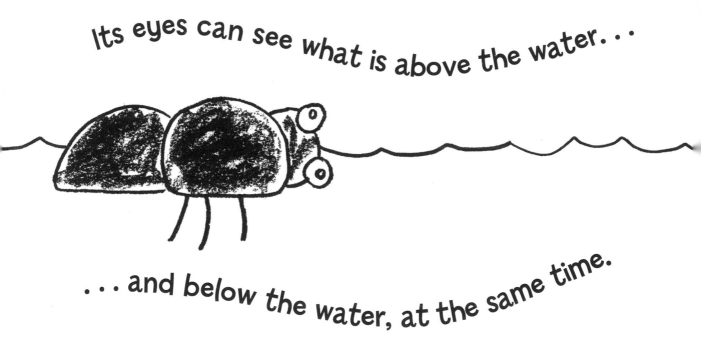

. . . and below the water, at the same time.

What can this whirligig beetle see?

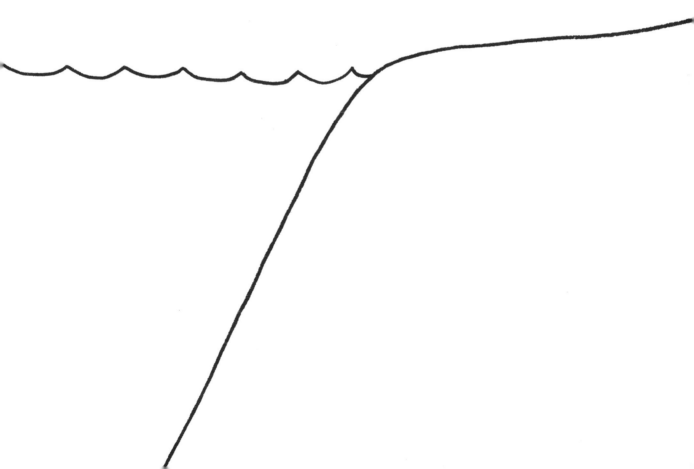

Some insects are so small,
you need a magnifying glass to see them.

What does this bug look like?

The body of an insect is split up into three parts. Each part has a name.

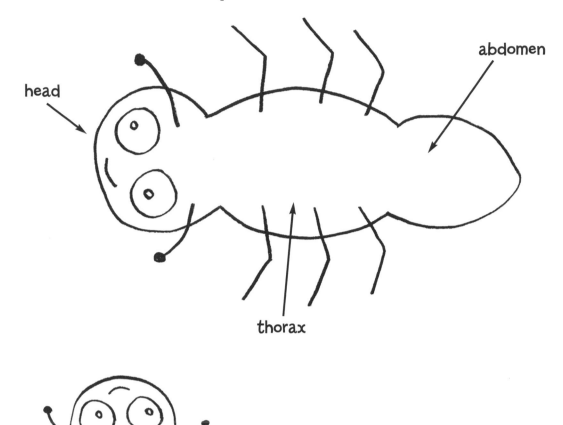

head

abdomen

thorax

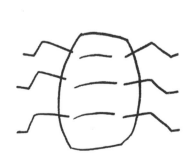

Can you complete these bugs?

Lots of bugs are nocturnal, which means they only come out at night.

What creepy crawlies are hiding in here?

Lots of bugs like dark, damp places.
What's living under this rock?

Earthworms live underground.

They are great at tunneling.

Fill the tunnels
with earthworms.

Scientists filled a rocket with spiders to see if they could spin webs in space.

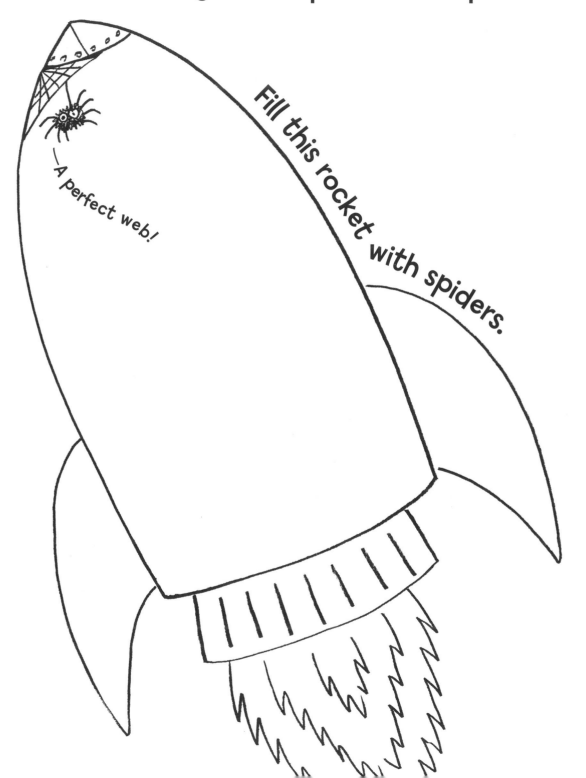

A perfect web!

Fill this rocket with spiders.

Some beetles roll dung, which is animal poo, into balls. Give these beetles some dung to roll.

I will eat my ball of dung.

I will sleep in mine.

Decorate these ladybugs.

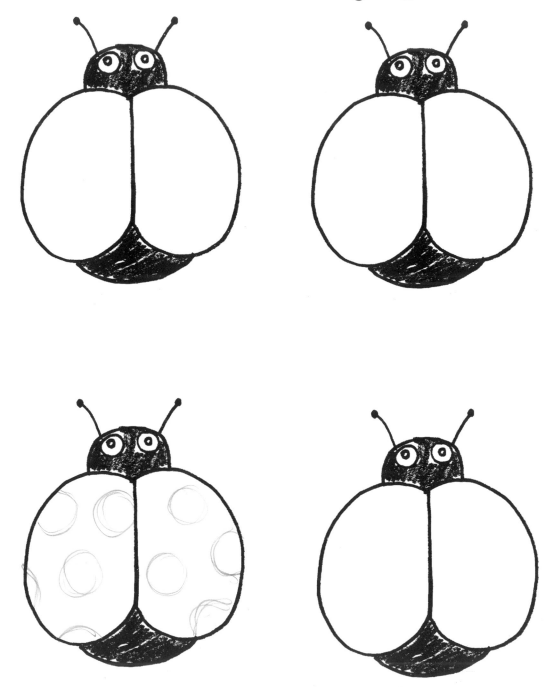

Some are red with black spots, some are
black and hairy. Some are red and yellow.

Some frogs catch bugs with their long, sticky tongues. What bug has this frog caught?

My tongue shoots out very fast – SPLAT!

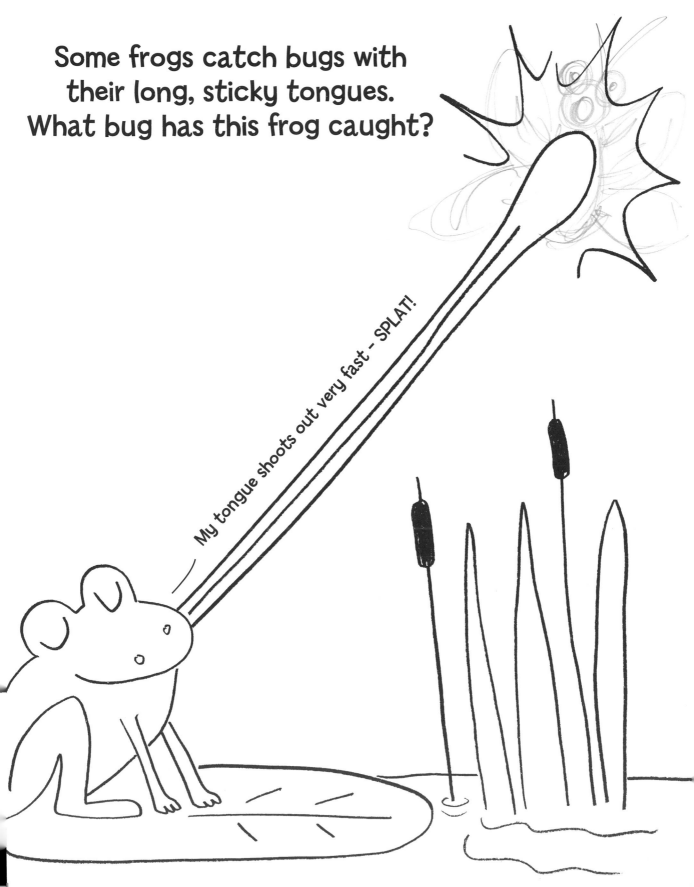

Caterpillars spend most of their time eating.

Fill the leaves with hungry caterpillars.

Munch, munch, munch.

Bees live together in a hive.
Fill this hive with bees.

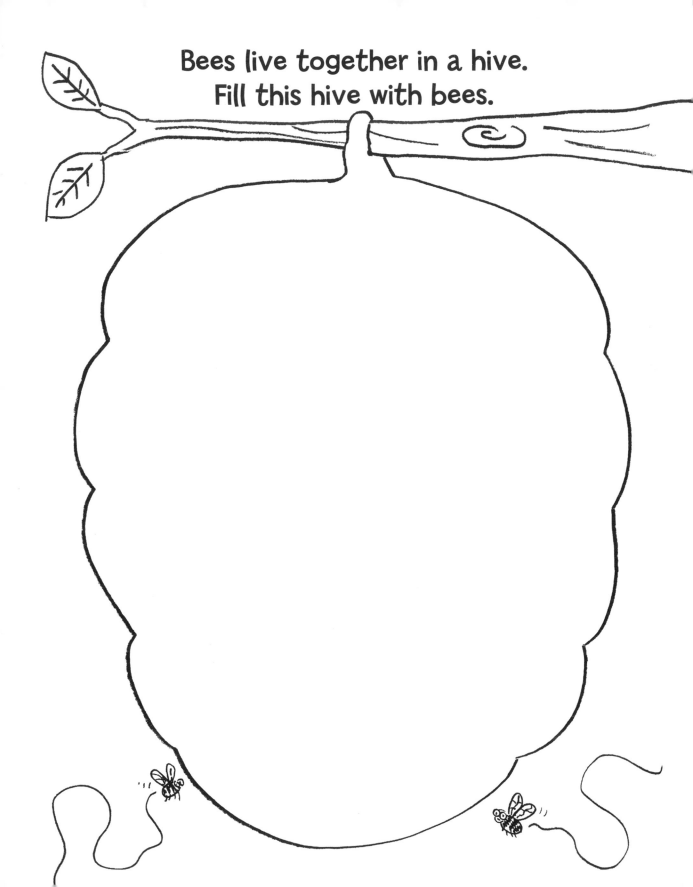

Most spiders eat insects they catch in their sticky webs. Fill this web with bugs.

There are around 20,000 different kinds of bees.
How many different kinds can you draw?

Many snails live in the water.
Add some to this underwater rock.

Centipedes have lots of legs. Some have over 100. How many legs can you add to this one?

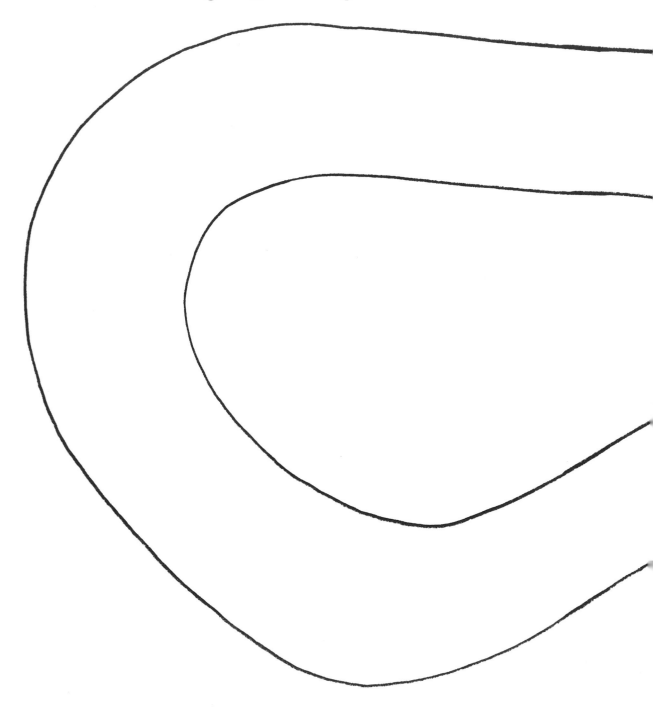

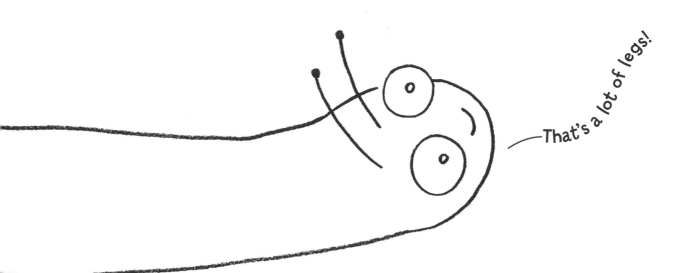

That's a lot of legs!

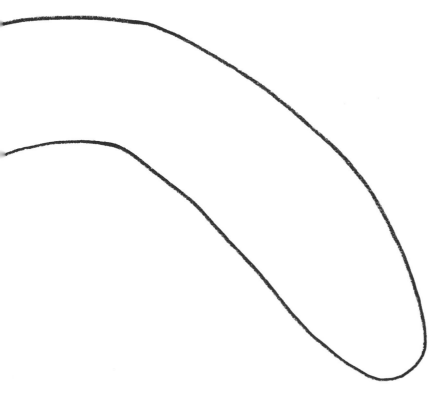

Bees make honeycomb. They store
their eggs and food for their eggs in it.
Can you finish this honeycomb?

Leeches look a bit like the slugs you find in the garden, but they like to suck blood!

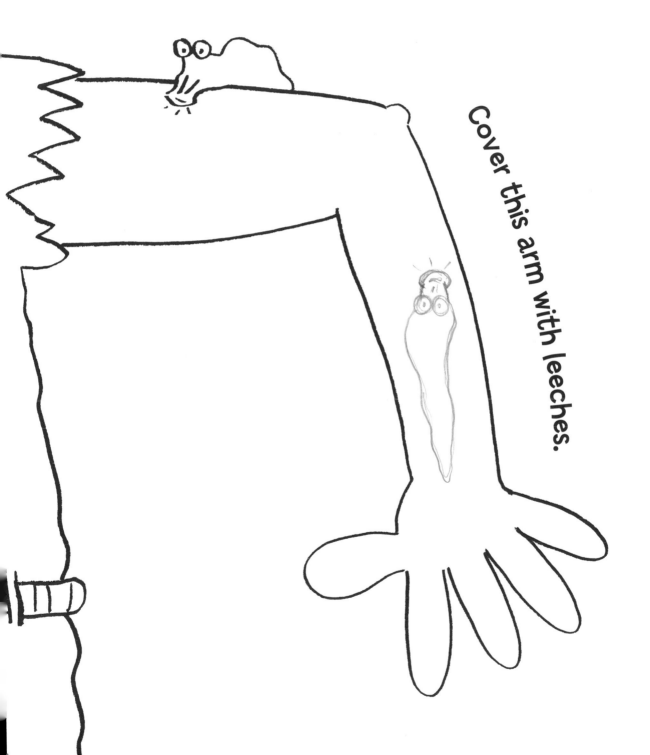

Cover this arm with leeches.

Caterpillars make cases called cocoons to live inside while they turn into butterflies. Hang cocoons from these branches.

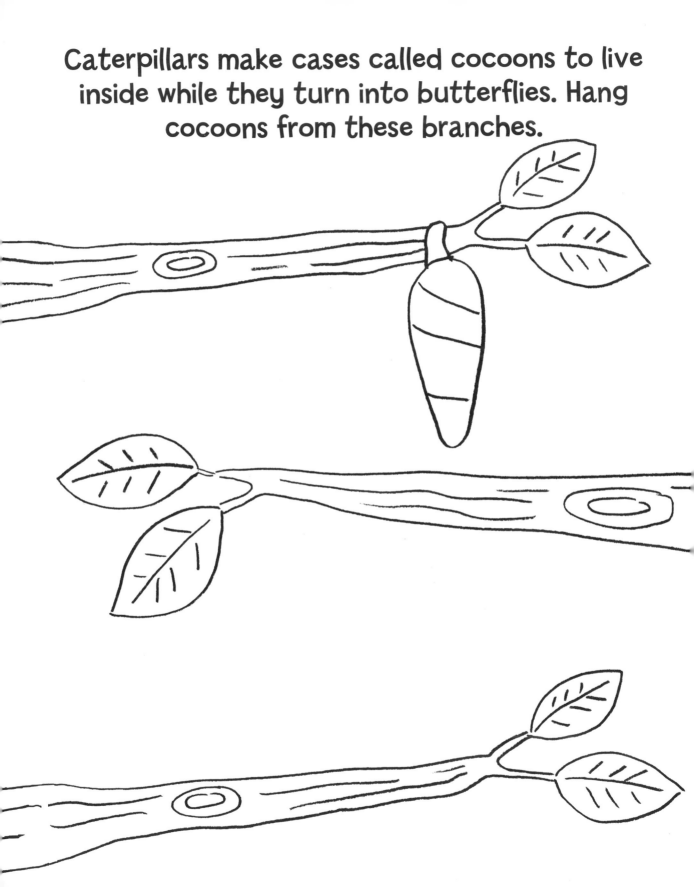

Wasps have yellow and black stripes.
Make these wasps stripy.

Some fleas have been trained to do funny tricks.

Fill this flea circus with performing fleas.

Some woodlice roll into balls to protect themselves. Make these balls into bugs.

Scientists know there are thousands of kinds of bugs they haven't discovered yet.

Create your very own bug in this jar.

Millions of years ago, there were giant dragonflies with huge wings.

Fill the swamp with giant dragonflies.

In winter, some butterflies fly to warmer countries. This is called migration.

Fill the sky with
migrating butterflies.

An ant can carry something that weighs
as much as 20 ants. What are they carrying?

A Venus flytrap is a plant that eats bugs.
If a bug lands on its leaves, the leaves close up,
trapping the bugs inside.

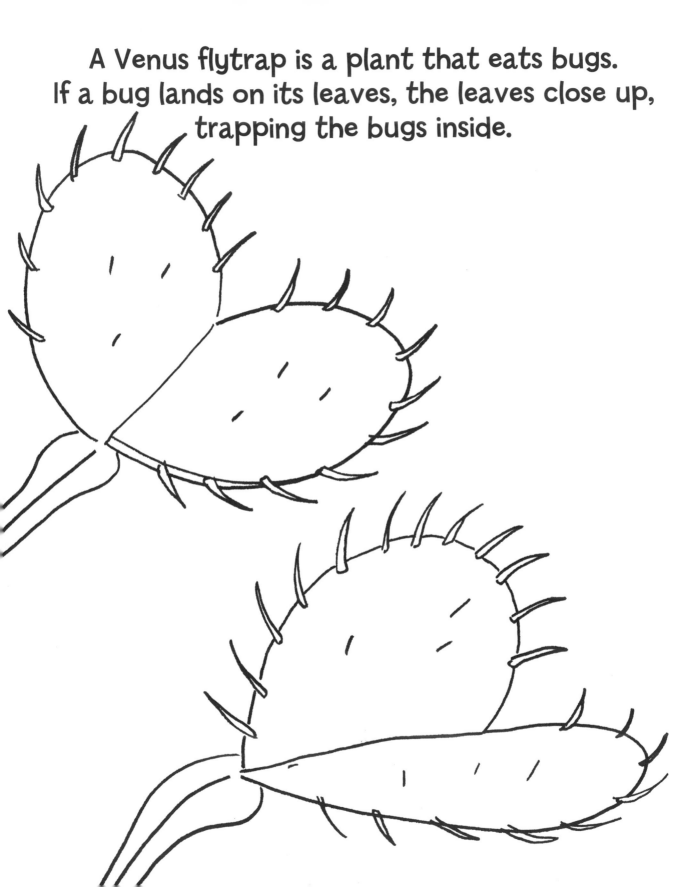

Give these plants some bugs to eat.

Stick insects are hard to see because they look like sticks.

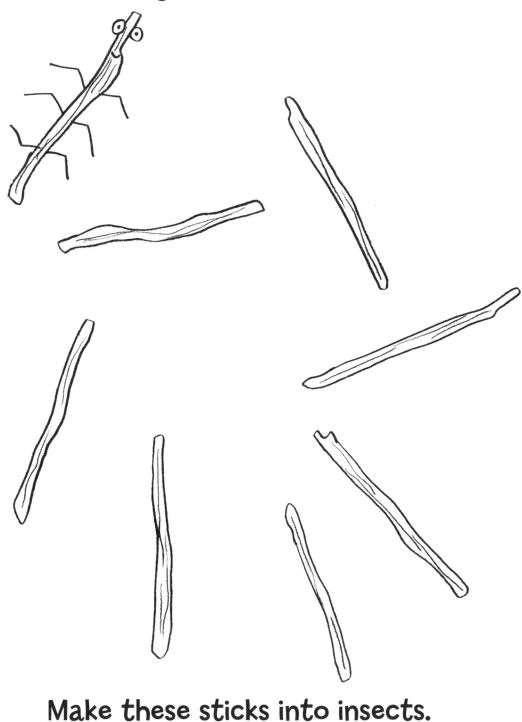

Make these sticks into insects.

Finish the web.

Bugs called pond skaters can walk on water.
Special hairs on their feet
help them to float.

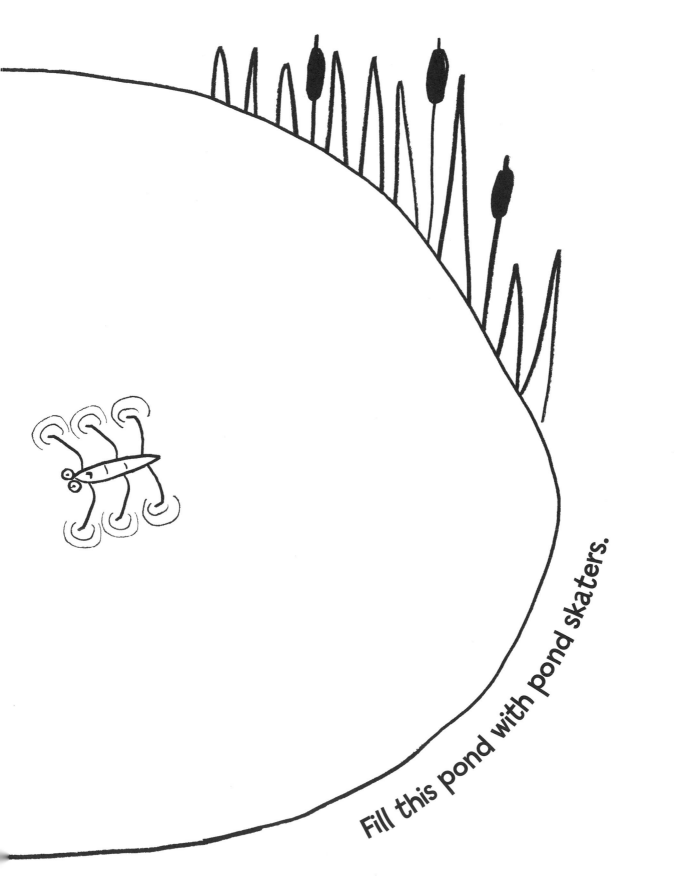

Fill this pond with pond skaters.

Scorpions' tails have deadly stings on them.
Give them all tails.

If a worm loses its tail, it can grow a new one.

Give these worms their tails back.

Millipedes have bodies made up of lots of bits, called segments.

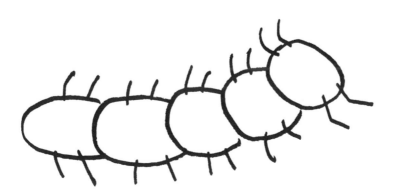

How many segments can you
add to this millipede?

In some countries, people eat bugs.

What is for dinner tonight?

Slugs leave a trail of slime behind them as they slide along.

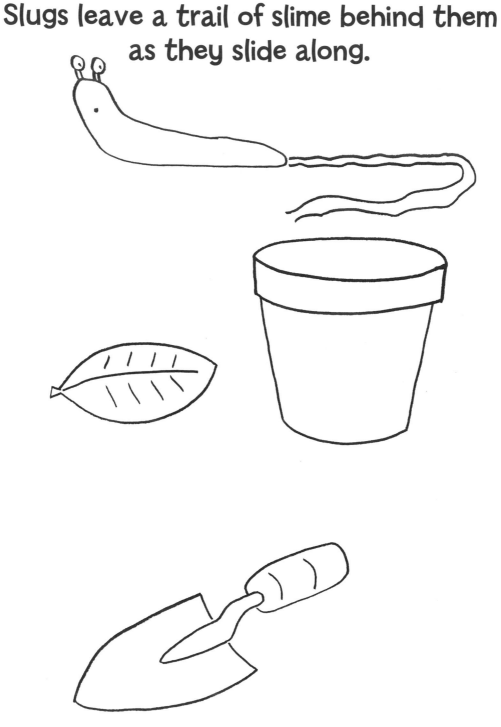

Finish the slug trail to find out where this slug has been.

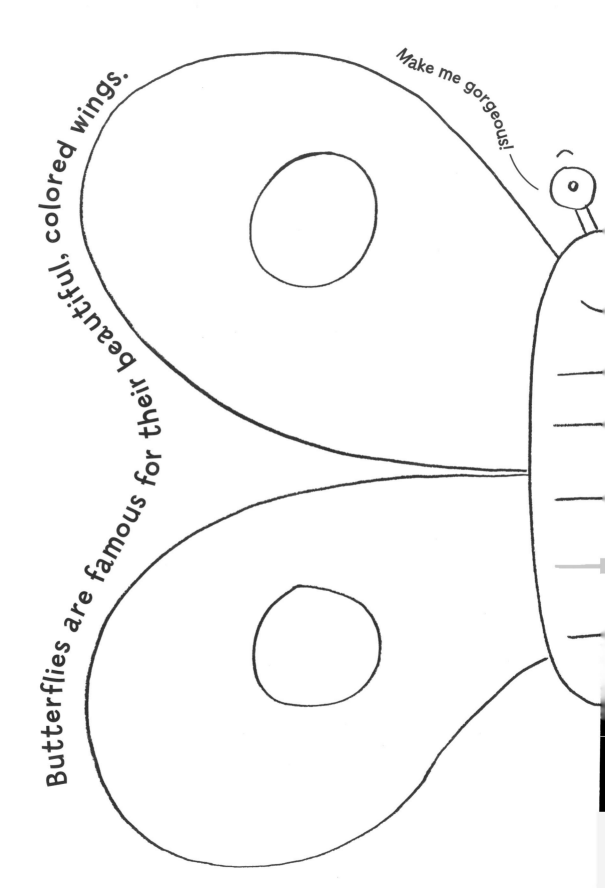

Butterflies are famous for their beautiful, colored wings.

Make me gorgeous!

Finish the butterfly's wings.

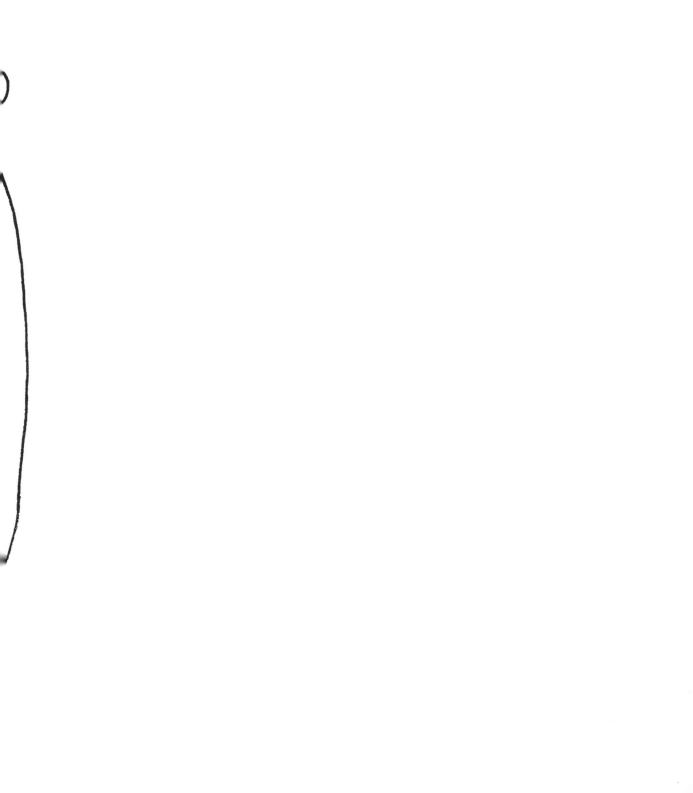

Headlice can lay their eggs in your hair.
The eggs are called nits.
Give this girl headlice and nits.